Ribboned pipefish

Purple queen anthias

Daisy parrotfish

Clown triggerfish

Broadclub cuttlefish

Dugong

Greater crested tern

Humpback grouper

Yellow-bellied sea snake

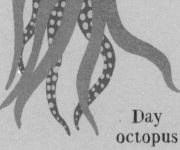
Day octopus

Yellow tang

Harlequin sweetlips

Pink anemonefish

Golden trevally

Royal blue tang

Picasso triggerfish

Copperband butterflyfish

Bird wrasse

Pennant coralfish

Spanish flag snapper

Red-footed booby

Green humphead parrotfish

Published in the US by Nobrow (US) Inc.
Printed in Poland on FSC® certified paper.

ISBN: 978-1-911171-41-6
Order from www.flyingeyebooks.com

Ella Bailey

ONE DAY
ON OUR
BLUE PLANET

...IN THE OCEAN

Flying Eye Books

London | New York

As day breaks, a little bottlenose dolphin calf takes a breath of fresh air, before diving back into the sparkling waters of the Pacific Ocean.

Below the surface, many more dolphins are swimming speedily. They all live, hunt and play together in a large group called a pod.

Just ahead, the little dolphin spots something... It's a baby whale, and he looks lost!

The little dolphin squeaks and clicks to her pod to draw their attention. Each dolphin has their own unique whistle, just like a name.

The little dolphin guides her new friend through the
warm shallow waters off the coast of Australia...

...and over the Great Barrier Reef where fish dart between the corals, and strange creatures lurk in secret crevices.

Once they reach the deep open ocean, the pod gathers together to protect the little dolphin and the baby whale.

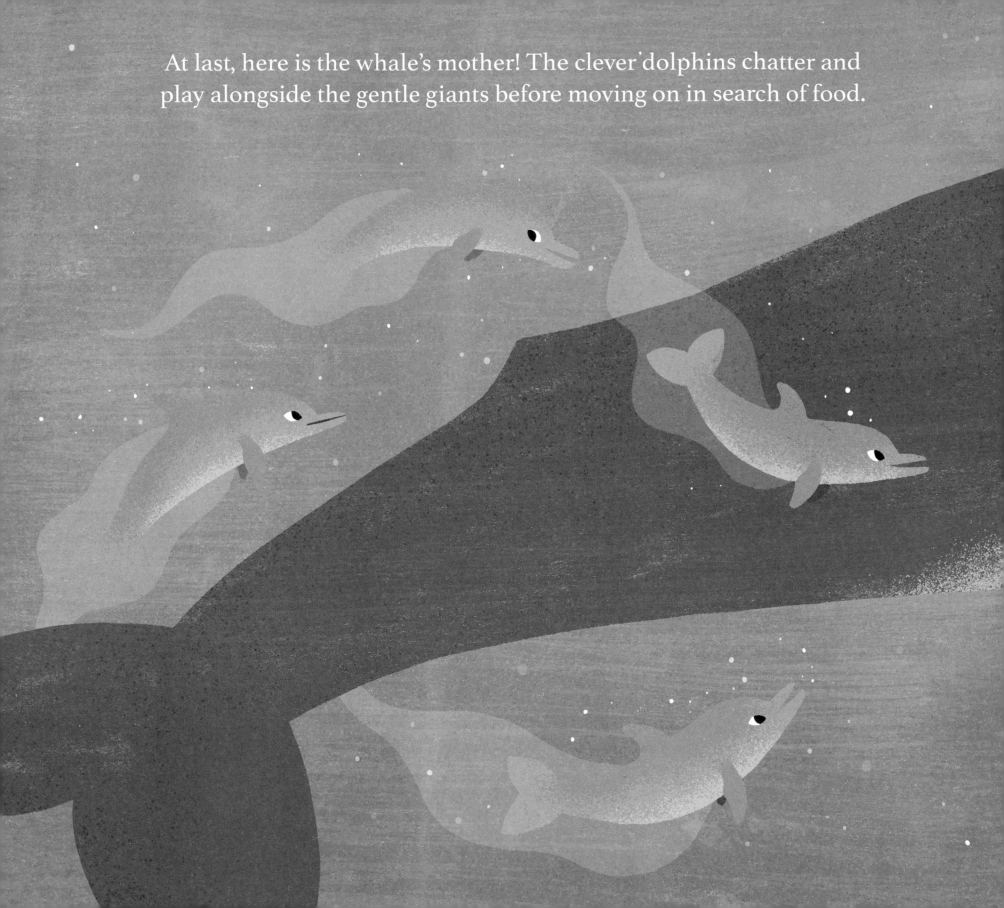

At last, here is the whale's mother! The clever dolphins chatter and play alongside the gentle giants before moving on in search of food.

Whales are not the only huge creatures living in this vast watery world. As she travels, the curious calf meets a strange ocean sunfish and a long lion's mane jellyfish...

...and a group of softly sweeping manta rays.

In the depths beyond, the pod sees a large shoal of fish. The older dolphins work together, grouping their prey near the surface so they are easy to catch.

The little dolphin likes fish, but like other baby mammals,
she also needs her mother's milk.

As night falls, the ocean grows darker and hungry sharks come out to hunt.

The little dolphin stays close by her mother's side, away from harm.

All dolphins must stay alert to breathe, so they sleep with one eye closed at a time. Together with her pod, the little dolphin swims sleepily through the glittering waters...

...until the sun rises again, on another day on our blue planet.

ANIMALS OF THE OCEAN
DEEP

Opah

Yellowfin tuna

Pilot fish

Pineapplefish

Swordfish

Wahoo

Bigfin reef squid

Blue mackerel

Rainbow runner

Red lionfish

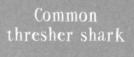

Common thresher shark

Blue whale

Epaulette shark

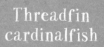

Threadfin cardinalfish